ROBERT CREELEY
If I were writing this

Also by Robert Creeley

POETRY

For Love • Words • The Charm • Pieces
A Day Book • Hello: A Journal • Later
Collected Poems: 1945–1975 • Mirrors
Memory Gardens • Selected Poems
Windows • Echoes • Life & Death
So There: Poems 1976–1983
Just in Time: Poems 1984–1994

FICTION

The Gold Diggers • The Island
Presences • Mabel: A Story
Collected Prose

DRAMA

Listen

ESSAYS

A Quick Graph: Collected Notes & Essays
Was That a Real Poem & Other Essays
Collected Essays
Autobiography
Tales Out of School

ANTHOLOGIES AND SELECTIONS

The Black Mountain Review 1954–1957
New American Story (with Donald M. Allen)
The New Writing in the U.S.A. (with Donald M. Allen)
Selected Writings of Charles Olson
Whitman: Selected Poems
The Essential Burns
Charles Olson, Selected Poems
George Oppen, Selected Poems

ROBERT CREELEY
If I were writing this

A NEW DIRECTIONS BOOK

Acknowledgments can be found on p. 103.

Design by Erik Rieselbach
Manufactured in the United States of America
New Directions Books are printed on acid-free paper.
First published clothbound by New Directions in 2003
Published simultaneously in Canada by Penguin Books Canada Ltd.

Library of Congress Cataloging-in Publication Data

Creeley, Robert, 1926–
If I were writing this / Robert Creeley.
p. cm.
ISBN 0-8112-1556-3 (cloth : alk. paper)
I. Title.
PS3505.R43I36 2003
811'.54—dc21   2003010672

New Directions Books are published for James Laughlin
by New Directions Publishing Corporation,
80 Eighth Avenue, New York, NY 10011

CONTENTS

for Pen, Will and Hannah

THE WAY

Somewhere in all the time that's passed
was a thing in mind became the evidence,
the pleasure even in fact of being lost
so quickly, simply that what it was could never last.

Only knowing was measure of what one could
make hold together for that moment's recognition,
or else the world washed over like a flood
of meager useless truths, of hostile incoherence.

Too late to know that knowing was its own reward
and that wisdom had at best a transient credit.
Whatever one did or didn't do was what one could.
Better at last believe than think to question?

There wasn't choice if one had seen the light,
not of belief but of that soft, blue-glowing fusion
seemed to appear or disappear with thought,
a minute magnesium flash, a firefly's illusion.

Best wonder at mind and let that flickering ambience
of wondering be the determining way you follow,
which leads itself from day to day into tomorrow,
finds all it ever finds is there by chance.

THE AMERICAN DREAM

Edges and disjuncts, shattered, bitter planes,
a wedge of disconsolate memories to anchor fame,
fears of the past, a future still to blame—

Multiple heavens, hells, nothing is straight.
You earn your money, then you wait
for so-called life to see that you get paid.

Tilt! Again it's all gone wrong.
This is a heartless, hopeless song.
This is an empty, useless song.

NAMES

Marilyn's was Norma Jean.
Things are not always what they seem.
Skin she lived back of like some screen

kept her wonder in common view,
said what she did, you could too,
loved by many, touched by few.

She married heroes of all kinds
but no one seemed to know her mind,
none the secret key could find.

Scared kid, Norma Jean?
Are things really what they seem?
What is it that beauty means?

TWENTY-FIVE

Balling the Jack   Down the Track
Won't Be Back   Too Late, Jack

See the rush of light—
Time's flight, out of sight.

Feel the years like tears—
the days gone away.

(LEMONS) PEAR APPEARS

If it's there, it's something—
And when you see it,
Not just your eyes know it.
It's yourself, like they say, you bring.

These words, these seemingly rounded
Forms—looks *like* a pear? *Is* yellow?
Where's *that* to be found—
In some abounding meadow?

Like likes itself, sees similarities
Everywhere it goes.
But what that means,
Nobody knows.

DRIED ROSES

"Dried roses..." Were these from some walk
All those years ago? Were you the one
Was with me? Did we talk?
Who else had come along?

Memory can stand upright
Like an ordered row of stiff stems,
Dead echo of flowering heads,
Roses once white, pink and red.

Back of them the blackness,
Backdrop for all our lives,
The wonders we thought to remember
Still life, still life.

DRAWN & QUARTERED

(1)

Speed is what's needed.
Move quick before depleted
of more than a battered leg will prove.
Go for it—as in love.

(2)

Hold still, lion!
I am trying
to paint you
while there's time to.

(3)

We have common sense
and common bond.
That's enough
to get along.

(4)

Have you known each other long?
Long before you were born!
Have you both been happy in marriage?
I think it's proven a commodious carriage.

(5)

Are they together?
Grandmother and granddaughter?
Is there some fact of pain
in their waiting?

(6)

Am I only material
for you to feel?
Is that all you see
when you look at me?

(7)

Image of self at earlier age—
when thoughts had gone inward,
and life became an emptying page—
myself moving toward nothing.

(8)

Why not tell
what you've kept a secret
not wait for it
to leap out?

(9)

Dear cat, I see you
and will attend
and feed you
now as then.

(10)

Here I sit
meal on lap
come to eat
just like that!

(11)

There's someone
behind
black eye covers,
smothered.

(12)

Closes, as an echo—
The shoulder, mouth, rounded
head—Two more, to say
each wanted it that way?

(13)

We sat like this
the night we went away—
just us two, in this same place,
and the boat on the ocean blue.

(14)

For years I'd thought
such bliss as this could not be bought.
While I waited,
my desire itself abated.

(15)

Something hot to drink.
God knows what's in it.
Waking or sleeping
in no one's keeping.

(16)

You displaced me by your singing.
My ears were ringing!
My fingers were glue
as each note rang true.

(17)

"Man, this stuff
is rough!"
"What would you pay
to make it go way?"

(18)

Still asleep or else dead.
Take him to bed.
He'll wake up in the morning
and I'll be gone.

(19)

Angel holding up
the roof top—
else would fall
and kill us all!

(20)

One word
    I heard
you said
    you read.

(21)

Mabel had come
all the way to town
to stand as you see her
and jump up and down.

(22)

Mine it was
and mine it will be—

No *because*
and never a *maybe*!

*Mine it was
and mine it will be...*

(23)

My only horse is dead,
who was my whole farmstead,
its entire provenance and agent.
Life has no further occasion.

(24)

Beyond, I hope, desire—
free of the entangling fire—
I lay me down to sleep.
Read it and weep!

(25)

"Too deep for words"—
My weary hand was poised
Above the paper's blank—
too white for thoughts, recalcitrant for tears.

(26)

What a complicated argument,
whether wrong or right!
Where's the fun
in being simply one?

(27)

He says the enemy's won—
and we can go home!
The drum beats
in the empty street.

(28)

Somewhere here it said
that *life is like a river*—
but look as hard as I can, I never
find it again—or anything else instead.

(29)

And have you read
my verses clear
and may I now
call you *my dear*?

(30)

All these pages
to turn,
all the bridges
to burn.

(31)

What I do
Is my own business.
No use looking.
You'll see nothing.

(32)

If music be
enough for you
lend me ears
so I can hear too.

(33)

Let me try that too
and see if I sound like you—
or is it your body's song
pulls things along?

(34)

When you are done
we can play!
Outside the day waits
until the sun goes down.

(35)

Oh little one,
what are you eating?
Bottle emptied beside you,
nought left but your thumb?

(36)

It was still in front of them
but soon began to be gone.
Look, said one, now it's going!
Still, they thought, it will come again.

(37)

Statue? Hermione's—
A Winter's Tale—
in the garden fixed
sense of beauty's evident patience.

(38)

Maybe this uniform's better,
Maybe this time I'll be the winner.
Maybe I'll shoot straighter.
Maybe they'll get dead first.

(39)

From the wars I've come,
following the drum,
cannon's bombast,
the military brass asses.

(40)

Love's the other
in the tunnel—
looks back
down the track.

(41)

Mother of her country,
keeping the dullards at bay,
forcing the boys to pay,
taking the fences away.

(42)

It's two o'clock
but we can't stop!
We couldn't then
when we drank the gin.

(43)

If I had a cent you'd have it.
But I don't.
If I knew what to do,
I'd tell you.

(44)

Your thought of me is so dear.
All I feel clears
in your own warm heart
and your eyes opened wide.

(45)

No animal would undertake
such a foolish isolation,
need to forgo a common dinner
so as not to be a common sinner.

(46)

Your cut, friend.
Is it, then?
Will you cheat again?
Let's see who wins.

(47)

On such a night,
as I may have told you,
the moon shone bright
and I grew older.

(48)

What will you shoot with that?
A rabbit!
Well, where will you find it?
Behind you!

(49)

The tea's cold,
cups still on other table.
The house is quiet
with no one inside it.

(50)

Like a circle,
uncoiling like a spring,
up and down and then around,
stairs are resourceful.

(51)

Summer's over?
Where was I
when it first came
bringing such pleasure?

(52)

"Miles to go"
but no snow
at least nor is it too long
till I'm safe at home.

(53)

Here browse the cows.
The gentle herdsman stands apart.
So nature's provenance
attends its art.

(54)

Finally to have come
to where one had so long wanted to visit
and then to stand
there and look at it.

LIFE

for Gael

Where have we drifted,
Or walked and talked our way into,
When it was attention we both thought to offer
All that we came to?

I can see you with your wee brush poised
To make the first crucial dab
Will encompass the wondering desert,
Marveling to find such witness.

Seriousness is its own reward?
It wasn't ever innocence,
Or a diffidence or indifference.
Not timidity ever.

Comment allez-vous, mate?
Like the last Canadian
Learned French at last to
Make friends too late?

But you had left long ago
And as all here I missed you,
Still acknowledging friend of my life,
Still true.

MILLAY'S ECHOES

"All I could see from where I stood
Was three long mountains and a wood;
I turned and looked the other way,
And saw three islands in a bay.
So with my eyes I traced the line
Of the horizon, thin and fine,
Straight around till I was come
Back to where I'd started from;
And all I saw from where I stood
Was three long mountains and a wood..."

Was three long mountains and a wood...
The emptying disposition stood,
The empty, echoing mind struck dumb,
The body's loss of kingdoms come,
Of suns, too many, long gone down,
And on that place precise she'd stood
Little was left to tell of time
Except the proof she *traced a line*
To make a poem *so with my eyes...*
of the horizon, thin and fine...

The circle held and here again
One sees what then she'd pointed to—
"Three islands in a bay," she said,
Much like that emptiness she knew,
The vaguest light, the softest mist
Hid them from sight. So fades at last
Whatever water will know best.
All proof seems pointless in such world,
Seems painful now to bring to mind.

Yet how forget that she once stood
Where now I do in altering time
And saw three mountains and a wood,
And pounding surf far down below
Where, when I look to see in kind
"The three long mountains and a wood,"
They are still there and still the sea
Beats back to me this monody.

FOR HANNAH'S FOURTEENTH BIRTHDAY

What's heart to say
as days pass,
what's a mind to know
after all?

What's it mean to be wise
or right,
if time's still
insistent master?

But if you doubt the track,
still don't look back.
Let the love you bring
find its fellow.

Girl to young woman,
world's well begun.
All comes true
just for you.

Trust heart's faith
wherever it goes.
It still knows
you follow.

FOR WILL

I was at the door,
still standing as if waiting for more—
but not knowing what for.

Was I with you?
Already we'd come a long distance together.
It was time now for something other.

In my head a story echoed
someone had told me
of how a son and father

came to a like doorway.
Then, in seeming anger, the son dragged the father out,
through an orchard, until the father shouted,

"Only this far *I* dragged *my* father! No more!
Put me down..." Was this to be their parting,
the last word? Was it only to be *gone*

each could think of, then, as each other?
All their time together, silent, warm,
knowing without thinking one another's mind,

no end to such—
could there be?
No, there was no end to it.

Always life was the constant
and one held it, gave it
one to another,

saw it go in that instant,
with love,
with all that one knows.

No riddle to that
except there is no end until it comes,
no friends but those one's found.

"WILD NIGHTS, WILD NIGHTS"

It seemed your friend
Had finally others to attend.
My time was yours alone to spend.

I leaned against the fence and waited.
Our love, I felt, was unequivocally fated.
To go sans word would leave all still unstated.

Hence scurrying hopes and pledge at last! Now here—
With all the fading years
Between—I wonder where

Time ever was before we
Walked in those towering woods, beneath the ample clouds,
Bathed in that wondrous air!

"WHEN I HEARD THE LEARN'D ASTRONOMER..."

for Allen

A bitter twitter,
flitter,
of birds
in evening's
settling,
a reckoning
beckoning,
someone's getting
some sad news,
the birds gone to nest,
to roost
in the darkness,
asking no improvident questions,
none singing,
no *hark,*
no *lark,*
nothing in the quiet dark.

Begun with like hypothesis,
arms, head, shoulders,
with body state
better soon than late,
better not wait,
better not be late,
breathe ease,
fall to knees
in posture of compliance,
obeisance,
accommodation
a motivation.

All systems must be imagination
which works,
albeit have quirks.

Add by the one
or by the none,
make it by *either*
or *or.*
Or say that after you
I go.
Or say you
follow me.
See what comes after
or before,
what
you had thought.

Many's a twenty?
A three?
Is twenty-three
plenty?

A call to reason
then
in due season,
a proposal of heaven
at seven
in the evening,
a cup of tea, a sense
of recompense
for anyone works for a living,
getting and giving.

Does it seem mind's all?
What's it mean
to be inside
a circle, to fly
in the sky, dear bird?

Words scattered,
tattered,
yet
said
make it
all evident,
manifest.
No contest.
One's one again.
It's done.

Hurry on, friend.
There is no end
to desire,
to Blake's fire,
to Beckett's mire,
to any such whatever.

Old friend's dead
in bed.

Old friends die.
Goodbye!

"WHERE LATE THE SWEET BIRDS SANG..."

for Don

Blunted efforts as the distance
Becomes insistent,
A divided time between now and then,
Between oneself and old friend—

Because what I'd thought age was,
Was a lessening, a fading
Reach to something not clearly seen,
But there still in memory.

No one thought it could be fun.
But—*Well begun is half done?*
Half gone, then it's all gone,
All of it over.

Now no one seems there anymore.
Each day, which had been a pleasure,
Becomes a fear someone else is dead,
Someone knocking at the door.

Born very young into a world already very old...
Always the same story
And I was told.
So now it's for me.

II

EN FAMILLE

for Ellie

I wandered lonely as a cloud...
I'd seemingly lost the crowd
I'd come with, family—father, mother, sister and brothers—
fact of a common blood.

Now there was no one,
just my face in the mirror, coat on a single hook,
a bed I could make getting out of.
Where had they gone?

     .

What was that vague determination
cut off the nurturing relation
with all the density, this given company—
what made one feel such desperation

to get away, get far from home, be gone from those
would know us even if they only saw our noses or our toes,
accept with joy our helpless mess,
taking for granted it was part of us?

     .

My friends, hands on each other's shoulders,
holding on, keeping the pledge
to be for one, for all, a securing center,
no matter up or down, or right or left—

to keep the faith, keep happy, keep together,
keep at it, so keep on
despite the fact of necessary drift.
Home might be still the happiest place on earth?

.

You won't get far by yourself.
It's dark out there.
There's a long way to go.
The dog knows.

It's him loves us most,
or seems to, in dark nights of the soul.
Keep a tight hold.
Steady, we're not lost.

.

Despite the sad vagaries,
anchored in love, placed in the circle,
young and old, a round—
love's fact of this bond.

One day one will look back
and think of them—
where they were, now gone—
remember it all.

.

Turning inside as if in dream,
the twisting face I want to be my own,
the people loved and with me still,
I see their painful faith.

Grow, dears, then fly away!
But when the dark comes, then come home.
Light's in the window, heart stays true.
Call—and I'll come to you.

    ·

The wind blows through the shifting trees
outside the window, over the fields below.
Emblems of growth, of older, younger,
of towering size or all the vulnerable hope

as echoes in the image of these three
look out with such reflective pleasure,
so various and close. They stand there,
waiting to hear a music they will know.

    ·

I like the way you both look out at me.
Somehow it's sometimes hard to be a human.
Arms and legs get often in the way,
making oneself a bulky, awkward burden.

Tell me your happiness is simply true.
Tell me I can still learn to be like you.
Tell me the truth is what we do.
Tell me that care for one another is the clue.

．

We're here because there's nowhere else to go,
we've come in faith we learned as with all else.
Someone once told us and so it is we know.
No one is left outside such simple place.

No one's too late, no one can be too soon.
We comfort one another, making room.
We dream of heaven as a climbing stair.
We look at stars and wonder why and where.

．

Have we told you all you'd thought to know?
Is it really so quickly now the time to go?
Has anything happened you will not forget?
Is where you are enough for all to share?

Is wisdom just an empty word?
Is age a time one might finally well have missed?
Must humanness be its own reward?
Is happiness this?

FOR YOU

At the edge, fledgling,
hypocrite reader, *mon frere,*
mon semblable, there
you are me?

CONVERSION TO HER

Parts of each person,
Lumber of bodies,
Heads and legs
Inside the echoes—

I got here slowly
Coming out of my mother,
Herself in passage
Still wet with echoes—

Little things surrounding,
Little feet, little eyes,
Black particulars,
White disparities—

Who was I then?
What man had entered?
Was my own person
Passing pleasure?

My body shrank,
Breath was constricted,
Head confounded,
Tongue muted.

I wouldn't know you,
Self in old mirror.
I won't please you
Crossing over.

Knife cuts through.
Things stick in holes.
Spit covers body.
Head's left hanging.

Hole is in middle.
Little boy wants one.
Help him sing here
Helpless and wanting.

.

My odor?
My name?
My flesh?
My shame?

My other
than you are,
my way out—
My door shut—

In silence this
happens, in pain.

.

Outside is empty.

Inside is a house
of various size.

Covered with skin
one lives within.

Women are told
to let world unfold.

Men, to take it,
make or break it.

All's true
except for you.

     ·

Being human, one wonders at the others,
men with their beards and anger,

women with their friends and pleasure—
and the children they engender together—

until the sky goes suddenly black and a monstrous thing
comes from nowhere upon them

in their secure slumbers, in their righteous undertakings,
shattering thought.

One cannot say, *Be as women,*
be peaceful, then. The hole from which we came

isn't metaphysical.
The one to which we go is real.

Surrounding a vast space
seems boundless appetite

in which a man still lives
till he become a woman.

CLEMENTE'S IMAGES

(1)

Sleeping birds, lead me,
soft birds, be me

inside this black room,
back of the white moon.

In the dark night
sight frightens me.

(2)

Who is it nuzzles there
with furred, round-headed stare?

Who, perched on the skin,
body's float, is holding on?

What other one stares still,
plays still, on and on?

(3)

Stand upright, prehensile,
squat, determined,

small guardians of the painful
outside coming in—

in stuck-in vials with needles,
bleeding life in, particular, heedless.

(4)

Matrix of world
upon a turtle's broad back,

carried on like that,
eggs as pearls,

flesh and blood and bone
all borne along.

(5)

I'll tell you what you want,
to say a word,

to know the letters in yourself,
a skin falls off,

a big eared head appears,
an eye and mouth.

(6)

Under watery here,
under breath, under duress,

understand a pain
has threaded a needle with a little man—

gone fishing.
And fish appear.

(7)

If small were big,
if then were now,

if here were there,
if find were found,

if mind were all there was,
would the animals still save us?

(8)

A head was put
upon the shelf got took

by animal's hand and stuck
upon a vacant corpse

who, blurred, could nonetheless
not ever be the quietly standing bird it watched.

(9)

Not lost,
not better or worse,
much must of necessity depend on resources,
the pipes and bags brought with us

inside, all the sacks
and how and to what they are or were attached.

(10)

Everybody's child
walks the same winding road,

laughs and cries, dies.
That's "everybody's child,"

the one who's in between
the others who have come and gone.

(11)

Turn as one will, the sky will always be
far up above the place he thinks to dream as earth.

There float the heavenly
archaic persons of primordial birth,

held in the scan of ancient serpent's tooth,
locked in the mind as when it first began.

(12)

Inside I am the other of a self,
who feels a presence always close at hand,
one side or the other, knows another one
unlocks the door and quickly enters in.

Either as or, we live a common person.
Two is still one. It cannot live apart.

(13)

Oh, weep for me—
all from whom life has stolen

hopes of a happiness stored
in gold's ubiquitous pattern,

in tinkle of commodious, enduring money,
else the bee's industry in hives of golden honey.

(14)

He is safely put
in a container, head to foot,

and there, on his upper part, wears still
remnants of a life he lived at will—

but, lower down, he probes at that doubled sack
holds all his random virtues in a mindless fact.

(15)

The forms wait, swan,
elephant, crab, rabbit, horse, monkey, cow,
squirrel and crocodile. From the one
sits in empty consciousness, all seemingly has come

and now it goes, to regather,
to tell another story to its patient mother.

(16)

Reflection reforms, each man's a life,
makes its stumbling way from mother to wife—

cast as a gesture from ignorant flesh,
here writes in fumbling words to touch,

say, *how can I be,*
when she is all that was ever me?

(17)

Around and in—
And up and down again,

and far and near—
and here and there,

in the middle is
a great round nothingness.

(18)

Not metaphoric,
flesh is literal earth

turns to dust
as all the body must,

becomes the ground
wherein the seed's passed on.

(19)

Entries, each foot feels its own way,
echoes passage in persons,

holds the body upright,
the secret of thresholds, lintels,

opening body above it,
looks up, looks down, moves forward.

(20)

Necessity, the mother of invention,
father of intention,

sister to brother to sister, to innumerable others,
all one as the time comes,

death's appointment,
in the echoing head, in the breaking heart.

(21)

In self one's place defined,
in heart the other find.

In mind discover *I*,
in body find the sky.

Sleep in the dream as one,
wake to the others there found.

(22)

Emptying out
each complicating part,

each little twist of mind inside,
each clenched fist,

each locked, particularizing thought,
forgotten, emptying out.

(23)

What did it feel like
to be one at a time—

to be caught in a mind
in the body you'd found

in yourself alone—
in each other one?

(24)

Broken hearts, a curious round of echoes—
and there behind them the old garden

with its faded, familiar flowers,
where all was seemingly laced together—

a trueness of true,
a blueness of blue.

(25)

The truth is in a container
of no size or situation.

It has nothing
inside.

Worship—
Warship. Sail away.

AS IF

As if a feeling, come from nought,
Suspended time in fascinated concentration,
So that all the world therein became
Of that necessity its own reward—

I lifted to mind a piece
Of bright blue air and then another.
Then clouds in fluffy substance floated by.
Below I felt a lake of azure waited.

I cried, *Here,* here *I am—the only place I'll ever be...*
Whether it made a common sense or found a world,
Years flood their gate, the company dispersed.
This person still is me.

POSSIBILITIES

for Susan Rothenberg

What do you wear?
How does it feel
to wear clothes?
What shows
what you were or where?

This accident, accidental, person,
feeling out, feelings out—
outside the box one's in—
skin's resonances, reticent romances,
the blotch of recognition, blush?

It's a place one's going,
going out to, could reach
out just so far to be at the edge
of it all, there, no longer inside,
waiting, expectant, a confused thing.

One wanted skin to walk in,
be in. One wanted each leg to stand,
both hands to have substance,
both eyes to look out, recognize,
all of it, closer and closer.

Put it somewhere, one says.
Put it down. But it's not a thing
simply. It's all of it here,
all of it near and dear,
everywhere one is, this and that.

Inside, it could have been included.
There was room for the world.
One could think of it, even be simple, ample.
But not "multitudes," not that way *in*—
It's out, *out,* one's going. Loosed.

Still—wistful in heaven, happy in hell?
Sky was an adamant wall,
earth a compact of dirty places,
faces of people one used to know.
Air—smell, sound and taste—was still wonderful.

One dreamed of a thoughtless moment,
the street rushing forward, heads up.
One willed almost a wave of silence
to hear the voices underneath.
Each layer, each particular, recalled.

But now to be *here?*
Putting my hand on the table,
I watch it turn into wood,
Fibrous, veins like wood's grain,
But not that way separated—all one.

I felt a peace come back.
No longer needed to say what it was,
nothing left somehow to name only—
still was each each, all all,
evident mass, bulky sum, a complex accumulation?

My mother dying sat up, ecstatic,
coming out of the anesthetic, said,
"It's all free! *You don't have to pay
for any of it...*" It's there
if you can still get to it?

Come closer, *closer*. Come as near
as you can get. Let me know
each edge, each shelf of act,
all the myriad colors, all the shimmering presences,
each breath, finger of odor, echoed pin drop.

Adumbrate nature. Walk a given path.
You are as much its fact as any other.
You stand a scale far smaller than a tree's.
A mountain makes you literal as a pebble.
Look hard for what it is you want to see.

The sky seems in its heavens, laced with cloud.
The horizon's miles and miles within one's sight.
Cooling, earth gathers in for night.
Birds quiet, stars start out in the dark.
Wind drops. Thus life itself can settle.

Nothing's apart from all and seeing is
the obvious beginning of an act
can only bring one closer to the art
of *being* closer. So feeling all there is,
one's hands and heart grow full.

FOR ANYA

An "outside" was always what I wanted
to get to, the proverbial opening
in the clearing, plain church with massed,
seated persons, the bright water
dense with white caps and happy children.

Was I late, stupid, to arrive always
as *It's me!*—somehow still alone,
however I'd thought myself present,
muted the persistent self-concerns,
took requisite chances, trying to let go?

Evening's clouds seem a dynasty,
an end forever to such confusion.
Birds sing still at the edges of hearing.
Night settles itself comfortably
far—and once and for all—beyond me.

I think and therefore I am self-conscious.
There are no mirrors here to look into,
No answering reassurances one's sufficient.
The "outside" is empty but vast, I think.
It's everywhere around me and still there.

THERE (1)

I left the wagon far too soon—
too particular, too big
or small for my britches.

I got off too early,
was too impatient to get there
and didn't even know where I was going.

I wouldn't let the company
count me in, take me with them,
even to a clearly pleasant place.

One by one was for me a confusion.
It was *one* period
I wanted—just *me,* just you—no more.

How does one get back on, brother?
Wherever you're going is fine with me.
Anything I've got is yours and always was.

THERE (2)

for Doug Messerli

Well if ever,
Then when never—

House's round,
Sound's sound.

Here's where
Comes *there*

If you do,
They will too.

III

THINKING

for Alex

Thought feels the edges.
Just so far it was only yesterday?
So far it seems now till tomorrow.

Time isn't space.
Away for the day, one says—
gone fishing. Now and again.

The sounds echo in the quiet morning—
such faint edges of place, things, not yet quite seen.
But one knows the familiar presences.

The world will be as one left it,
still there, to reappear again perhaps
where it always is.

CAMBRIDGE, MASS 1944

Sister remembers
night she'd come down
to meet me in town
my friends then told her

I'd jumped in the river
and hadn't returned.
—But once in the water
I'd kept on swimming

across to far shore
where police fished me out
and put me in jail
where I stayed the night

naked in cell
so clothes could dry out.
Next morning the judge
gave me dime to get home.

PLACE TO BE

Days the weather sits
in the endless sky,
the clouds drifting by.

The winter's snow,
summer's heat,
same street.

Nothing changes
but the faces, the people,
all the things they do

'spite of heaven and hell
or city hall—
Nothing's wiser than a moment.

No one's chance
is simply changed by wishing,
right or wrong.

What you do is how you get along.
What you did is all it ever means.

PICTURES

for Pen

(1)

This distance
between pane of glass,
eye's sight—
the far waving green edge

of trees, sun's
reflection, light
yellow—and sky there too
light blue.

(2)

I will sit here
till breeze, ambient,
enfolds me and I
lift away. I will

sit here as sun
warms my hands, my
body eases, and sounds
grow soft and intimate

in my ears. I will sit
here and the back of the house
behind me will at last
disappear. I will sit here.

(3)

Harry's gone out for pizza.
Mabel's home all alone.
Mother just left for Ibiza.
Give the old man a bone?

Remember when Barkis was willing?
When onions grew on the lawn?
When airplanes cost just a shilling?
Where have the good times gone?

(4)

If one look back
or thinks to look
in that uselessly opaque direction,
little enough's ever there.

What is it one stares into,
thinks still to recover
as it all fades out—
mind's vagary?

I call to you brutally.
I remember the day we met
I remember how you sat, impatient
to get out.

Back is no direction...
Toute passe?
Life is the river
we've carried with us.

(5)

Sun's shadows aslant
across opening expansive
various green fields down

from door
here ajar on box tower's
third floor—

look out on
wonder.
This morning.

(6)

I never met you afterward
nor seemingly knew you before.

Our lives were interfolded,
wrapped like a present.

The odors, the tastes, the surfaces
of our bodies were the map—
the mind a distraction,
trying to keep up.

I could not compare you to anything.
You were not like rhubarb
or clean sheets—or, dear as it might be,
sudden rain in the street.

All those years ago, on the beach in Dover,
with that time so ominous,
and the couple so human,
pledging their faith to one another,

now again such a time seems here—
not to fear
death or what's been so given—
to yield one's own despair.

(7)

Like sitting in back seat,
can't see what street
we're on or what the
one driving sees

or where we're going.
Waiting for what's to happen,
can't quite hear the conversation,
the big people, sitting up front.

(8)

Death, be not proud...
Days be not done.
Air be not gone.
Head be not cowed.

Bird be not dead.
Thoughts be not fled.
Come back instead,
Heart's hopeful wedding.

Face faint in mirror.
Why does it stay there?
What's become
Of person who was here?

(9)

Wet
      water
warm
      fire.

Rough
      wood
cold
      stone.

Hot
      coals
shining
      star.

Physical hill still my will.
Mind's ambience alters all.

(10)

As I rode out one morning
just at break of day
a pain came upon me
unexpectedly—

As I thought one day
not to think anymore,
I thought again,
caught, and could not stop—

Were I the horse I rode,
were I the bridge I crossed,
were I a tree
unable to move,

the lake would have
no reflections,
the sweet, soft air
no sounds.

So I hear, I see,
tell still the echoing story
of all that lives in a forest,
all that surrounds me.

SUPPER

Shovel it in.
Then go away again.
Then come back and
shovel it in.

Days on the way,
lawn's like a shorn head
and all the chairs are put away
again. Shovel it in.

Eat for strength, for health.
Eat for the hell of it, for
yourself, for country and your mother.
Eat what your little brother didn't.

Be content with your lot
and all you got.
Be whatever they want.
Shovel it in.

I can no longer think of heaven
as any place I want to go,
not even dying. I want
to shovel it in.

I want to keep on eating,
drinking, thinking.
I am ahead. I am not dead.
Shovel it in.

"SHORT AND CLEAR"

for Gregory, who said it

Short and clear, dear—
short and clear.

No need for fear.
All's here.

Keep it
short and clear.

You are the messenger,
the message, the way.

Short and clear, dear,
all the way.

SCHOLAR'S ROCKS

for Jim Dine

(1)

What has been long pondered,
become encrusted,
grown into itself—

colored by world, by echoed
independence from world,
by all that it wasn't—

what had been thought,
what had been felt,
what was it?

(2)

As in a forest
as if   *as if*
one had come to

as in a forest
to a wall of the heart

a wall
of the heart

(3)

glass
enclosing including

stuck into
these insistent

Things

(4)

Ghosts of
another *wall*—

childhood's—
all hung

in order
elegant and particular

hands   handed
hand tools

(5)

What happens when
the house is at last
quiet and the lights
lowered, go finally out?

Then is it all silent?
Are the echoes still,
the reflections faded,
the places left alone?

(6)

As fingers round a stick,
as a pen's held,
a thumb can help grip,
so a wrench's extension,

a hammer's force,
meticulous cutting clippers,
hatchet's sharpened edge
one could not cut without.

(7)

I love the long wrench,
whose gears permit a tension
'twixt objects fixed
tight between its iron teeth.

So locked, one can twist
and so the object turns,
loosens, at last comes out.
This is life's bliss!

(8)

Which
one
did
it?

Do you recognize
the culprit,
is your own heart
full?

(9)

Sometimes it's like looking at orphans—
and no one will come.

No one seems to want them.
There's a patience, which seems awful—

inhuman to be left,
to have no place on earth?

The heart alone holds them.
Minds made them.

(10)

Seeing's believing. Beyond eyes, beyond the edges of things.
The face of what's out there is an adamant skin. One touches
it, feels it. Coming, going, *through the looking glass...* Leaving
marks, making a trail for the way back. One writes on the sur-
face, sensing all that's under it. Oceans of a common history.
Things of the past.

BUB AND SIS

for Carolyn Kizer

Let the dog lie down with the dog,
people with people.
It makes a difference where you fit
and how you feel.

When young, I was everybody's human,
a usual freaked person,
looking for love in the dark,
being afraid to turn the lights on.

It makes a great difference
to have a friend
who's a woman,
when you're a so-called man,

who can talk to you
across the great divide
of mixed signals
and wounded pride.

Small thanks in the end
for that maintaining sister,
but what she says
is what you remember.

FOR GEORG

Art says,
what are you looking at?

But the words want
to say what they have to.

If there is *here,*
then there's here *too?*

The grey green monster with
the ugly face isn't here,

the words want to say. But, *look,*
says the image, *right behind you!*

Anthropomorphic instance in any case
is a drag. You don't get reality as choices.

The battle goes on,
pens into ploughshares, canvas into awnings—

or simply faces
in the crowd. I want

a lot of things, the
separables, the x's and y's

of existence. *Upside down,*
says Georg, *is a whole new ballgame!*

The runner
advances to second.

FOR GREGORY CORSO

I'll miss you,
who did better than I did
at keeping the faith of poets,
staying true.

It's as if you couldn't
do otherwise,
had always an appetite
waiting to lead.

You kept to the high road
of canny vision,
let the rest of us
find our own provision.

Ruthless, friends felt,
you might take everything.
Nothing was safe from you.
You did what you wanted.

Yet, safe in your words, your poems,
their humor could hold me.
The wit, the articulate
gathering rhythms,

all made a common sense
of the archaic wonders.
You pulled from nowhere the kingly chair.
You sat alone there.

THE HEART

for Pen

In the construction
of the chest, there is
a heart.

A boat
upon its blood
floats past

and round or down
the stream of life,
the plummeting veins

permit its passage
to admit no gains,
no looking back.

One steps aboard,
one's off.
The ticket taker

signs the time allotted.
Seated, amorphous persons
see no scenery

but feel
a chill about their knees
and hear a fading cry

as all the many sides of life
whiz by,
a blast at best, a loss

of individual impressions.
Still I sit
with you inside me too—

and *us,*
the couple thus encoupled,
ride on into the sweetening dark.

MEMORY

for Keith and Rosmarie

Remember when
we all were ten
and had again
what's always been—

Or if we were,
no fear was there
to cause some stir
or be elsewhere—

Because it's when
all thoughts occur
to say again
we're where we were.

"IF I WERE WRITING THIS..."

If I were writing this
with prospect of encouragement
or had I begun some work
intended to be what it was

or even then and there it was what
had been started, even now
I no longer thought to wait,
had begun, had found

myself in the time and place
writing words which I knew,
could say *ring, dog, hat, car,*
was rushing, it felt, to keep up

with the trembling impulse,
the connivance the words contrived
even themselves to be though
I wrote them, thought they were me.

．

Once in, once out
Turn's a roundabout
Seeing eyes get the nod

Or dog's a mistaken god?
God's a mistaken dog?

Gets you home on time
Rhymes with time on time

In time for two a "t"
begins and ends it.

          .

A blue grey edge.
Trees line it.
Green field finds it.
Eyes look.

          .

Let the aching heart take over.
Cry till eyes blur.
Be as big as you were.
Stir the pot.

          .

Whenever it's sense,
look for what else is meant
in the underthought of language.
Words are apparent.

Seen light turns off
to be ambient luminescence,
there and sufficient.
No electricians.

          .

Same sight,
shadows at edge of light,
green field again
where hedgerow finds it.

Read these words then
and see the far trees,
hear the chittering of the birds,
share my ease and dependence.

FOR KENNETH

It was never a joke.
Hell's not its own reward.
If one even thought of it,
then there it was.

But your classic humor
of the edge, of being about to—
and hanging on even for one last look—
that was truly heroic.

I thought "Sleeping with Women"
sounded like birds settling
in some idyllic edge of meadow
just at night fall.

So there I held on—put my head
down on the pillow,
slept with your words recurring,
fast in their thought.

HICCUPS

for Phil

It all goes round,
nothing lost, nothing found—
a common ground.

Outside is in,
that's where it all begins
and where it seems to end.

An ample circle
with center full
of all that's in this world—

or that one—
or still another someone
else had thought was fun.

An echo, a genial emptiness,
a finally common place, a bliss
of this and this and this.

YESTERDAYS

Sixty-two, sixty-three, I most remember
As time W. C. Williams dies and we are
Back from a hard two years in Guatemala
Where the meager provision of being
Schoolmaster for the kids of the *patrones*
Of two coffee plantations has managed
Neither a life nor money. Leslie dies in
Horror of bank giving way as she and her
Sister and their friends tunnel in to make
A cubby. We live in an old cement brick
Farmhouse already inside the city limits
Of Albuquerque. Or that has all really
Happened and we go to Vancouver where,
Thanks to friends Warren and Ellen Tallman,
I get a job teaching at the University of British
Columbia. It's all a curious dream, a rush
To get out of the country before the sad
Invasion of the Bay of Pigs, that bleak use
Of power. One of my British colleagues
Has converted the assets of himself and
His wife to gold bullion and keeps the
Ingots in a sturdy suitcase pushed under
Their bed. I love the young, at least I
Think I do, in their freshness, their attempt
To find ways into Canada from the western
Reaches. Otherwise the local country seems
Like a faded Edwardian sitcom. A stunned
Stoned woman runs one Saturday night up
And down the floors of the Hydro Electric
Building on Pender with the RCMP in hot

Pursuit where otherwise we stood in long
Patient lines, extending often several blocks
Up the street. We were waiting to get our
Hands stamped and to be given a 12 pack
Of Molson's. I think, I dream, I write the
Final few chapters of *The Island,* the despairs
Gathering at the end. I read Richard Brautigan's
Trout Fishing In America but am too uptight
To enjoy his quiet, bright wit. Then that
Summer there is the great Vancouver Poetry
Festival, Allen comes back from India, Olson
From Gloucester, beloved Robert Duncan
From Stinson Beach. Denise reads "Hypocrite
Women" to the Burnaby ladies and Gary Snyder,
Philip Whalen, and Margaret Avison are there
Too along with a veritable host of the young.
Then it's autumn again. I've quit my job
And we head back to Albuquerque
And I teach again at the university, and
Sometime just about then I must have
Seen myself as others see or saw me,
Even like in a mirror, but could not quite
Accept either their reassuring friendship
Or their equally locating anger. Selfish,
Empty, I kept at it. Thirty-eight years later
I seem to myself still much the same,
Even if I am happier, I think, and older.

GROUND ZERO

What's after or before
seems a dull locus now
as if there ever could be more

or less of what there is,
a life lived just because
it is a life if nothing more.

The street goes by the door
just like it did before.
Years after I am dead,

there will be someone here instead
perhaps to open it,
look out to see what's there—

even if nothing is,
or ever was,
or somehow all got lost.

Persist, go on, believe.
Dreams may be all we have,
whatever one believe

of worlds wherever they are—
with people waiting there
will know us when we come

when all the strife is over,
all the sad battles lost or won,
all turned to dust.

JOHN'S SONG

for John Taggart

If ever there is
if ever, if ever
there is, if ever there is.

If ever there is
other than war, other
than where war was, if ever there is.

If ever there is
no war, no more war, no other than us
where war was, where it was.

No more war, dear brother,
no more, no more war
if ever there is.

EMPTINESS

for Helen

The emptiness up the field where
the barn sits still like an ark, an old
presence I look up there to see, sun
setting, sky gone a vivid streaking of
reds and oranges, a sunset off over the
skirt of woods where my sister's barn sits
up the field with all her determined stuff,
all she brought and put in it, all her
pictures, her pots, her particular books
and icons—so empty, it seems, quickly
emptied of everything there was in it, like
herself the last time in the hospital bed had
been put to face out the big window back of
tv, so one could look out, see down there,
over the field, trees of our place, the house,
woods beyond going off toward Warren, the sight,
she'd say with such emphasis, *I'm where I*
want to be!—could ever Maine be more loved,
more wanted, all our history trailing back
through its desperation, our small people, small
provision, where the poor folk come from like
us, to Massachusetts, to a world where poverty
was a class, like Mrs. Peavey told our mother
she'd never felt poor before, not till she was
given charity by the women of the Women's
Club, her family their annual recipient—empty,
empty, running on *empty,* on nothing, on heart,
on bits and pieces of elegance, on an exquisite frame

of words, on each and every memory she ever had,
on the same will as our mother's, the pinched privacy
of empty purse, the large show of pleasure, of out there
everything, come in, *come in*—she lay there so still,
she had gone into herself, face gone then but for echo
of way she had looked, no longer saw or heard, no more
of any human want, no one wanted. *Go away,*
she might have been saying, *I'm busy today.* Go away.
Hence then to be cremated, to reach the end and be done.

MEMORY

Somewhere Allen Ginsberg is
recalling his mother's dream
about God, *an old man,* she says,
*living across the river in
Palisades,* obscure, battered,
in a shack with hardly any
provisions. Straight off she asks him,
*how could you let the world get
into such a mess,* and he can
answer only, *I did the best I could.*
She tells Allen he looks neglected
and there are yellow pee-stains
on his underpants. Hard to hear
God could not do any better
than any of us, just another old
man sitting on some bench or some
chair. I remember it was a urologist
told me how to strip the remaining pee
from my penis by using my finger's
pressure just back of the balls,
the prostate, then bringing it forward
so that the last drops of it would go
into the toilet, not onto my clothes.
Still it's of necessity an imperfect
solution. How stand at a public urinal
seeming to play with oneself? Yet
how not—if that's what it takes not
to walk out, awkward, wide-legged, damp
from the crotch down? I cannot

believe age can be easy for anyone. *On
Golden Pond* may be a pleasant picture
of a lake and that general area of
New Hampshire, but it's not true,
any of it. Please, don't put, if
you can help it, your loved ones in
a care facility, they will only die there.
Everyone's sick there. It's why they've come.
I don't know now what will or
may happen to me. I don't
feel any longer a simple person with
a name. I am like a kid at his,
or her, first day of school. All new,
all surprising. The teacher with
her curious large face, the other
unexpected children, all of us finally
unsure. The seeming fractures of a self
grow ominous, like peaks of old
mountains remembered but faint
in the obscuring fog. Time to push off, do
some push-ups perhaps, take a walk with
the neighbors I haven't spoken to in years.

GENEROUS LIFE

Do you remember the way we used to sing
in church when we were young
and it was fun to bring your toys with you
and play with them while all the others sung?

My mind goes on its own particular way
and leaves my apparent body on its knees
to get up and walk as far as it can
if it still wants to and as it still proves able.

Sit down, says generous life, *and stay awhile!*
although it's irony that sets the table
and puts the meager food on broken dishes,
pours out the rancid wine and walks away.

INDEX

of titles (in capitals) and first lines

ACKNOWLEDGMENTS

Grateful thanks to the editors of those journals who first printed some of these poems, including *Conjunctions, Slate, The New Yorker, American Poetry Journal, Boston Review, Woodstock Journal, Exquisite Corpse, Jacket, Bridge, Butcher's Block, Can We Have Our Ball Back, Cairn, Colorado Review, Flash Point, Square One* and *The Café Review.*

Thanks also to those institutions and presses whose publications included my work, among them Backwood Broadsides (Maine), Drive He Said Press (New Mexico), Granary Books (New York), Guggenheim Museum (New York), Museum of Fine Arts (Boston), Memorial Art Gallery (Rochester, N.Y.), Museum Berg Wissem (Germany), Chax Press (Arizona), Z Press (Vermont), Museum of Modern Art (New York), Tamerind Institute (New Mexico), Naropa Institute (Colorado), Nation Books (New York), Marco Fine Arts (Los Angeles), Au Quai (Scotland) and Vennel Press (England).

Finally thanks to the Lannan Foundation, the Skowhegan School of Art and the Bogliasco Foundation for their various support, which much enabled the writing of this book.

R. C.